MADISKARTE

Strategic Thinking with the Law of Attraction in Mind

RIO CARANDANG

I dedicate this Book to God Almighty my Creator, my Strong Pillar, my Source of Inspiration, Wisdom, Knowledge and Understanding! Secondly, to my family who has always been there for me!

Table of Contents

FOREWORD 6

INTRODUCTION 9

WHAT IS *MADISKARTE?* 14

WHY STRATEGIC THINKING MATTERS 19

THE POWER OF THE LAW OF ATTRACTION 23

PART I: UNDERSTANDING THE LAW OF
ATTRACTION 26

The Basics of the Law of Attraction 30

The Science behind the Law of Attraction 34

The Law of Attraction and Your Thoughts 38

The Law of Attraction and Your Emotions 41

PART II: APPLYING THE LAW OF ATTRACTION IN
STRATEGIC THINKING 44

Defining Your Goals and Dreams 51

Creating a Vision Board for Your Goals 54

Visualizing Your Success 61

Taking Action with the Law of Attraction 65

PART III: STRATEGIES FOR *MADISKARTE* THINKING 69

Embracing Abundance Thinking 72

Overcoming Limiting Beliefs 76

Cultivating a Positive Mindset 80

Practicing Gratitude and Appreciation 84

Developing Resilience and Perseverance 88

PART IV: *MADISKARTE* THINKING IN ACTION 91

Madiskarte in Business and Entrepreneurship 95

Madiskarte in Career and Professional Development 98

Madiskarte in Personal Relationships 102

Madiskarte in Health and Wellness 105

CONCLUSION 112

The Power of *Madiskarte* 115

Putting *Madiskarte* into Practice 119

Embracing a *Madiskarte* Mindset 124

Foreword

The Law of Attraction has been a subject of interest for many people in recent years. It's no wonder why – the idea that we can manifest our desires through our thoughts and emotions is compelling, and many have experienced positive results from applying it in their lives. However, some people dismiss it as mere pseudoscience or wishful thinking, while others struggle to make it work for them.

That's where *"Madiskarte: Strategic Thinking with the Law of Attraction in Mind"* comes in. This book is a comprehensive guide to understanding and applying the Law of Attraction in a strategic way. It's not just about wishful thinking or positive affirmations – it's about using the Law of Attraction to set goals, create a vision, and take action towards achieving them.

The author presents a clear and practical approach to the Law of Attraction. He emphasizes the importance of mindset, emotions, and visualization, but also provides concrete strategies for overcoming limiting beliefs, developing resilience, and taking consistent action.

What sets this book apart from other Law of Attraction books is its focus on *"Diskarte"* – a Filipino term that means being "resourceful" or "clever." The author shows how *Madiskarte* thinking can enhance the Law of Attraction by leveraging creativity, adaptability, and a positive attitude. This *Madiskarte* principle can be applied in various areas of life, from business and career to personal relationships and health.

I believe that *"Madiskarte: Strategic Thinking with the Law of Attraction in Mind"* is a resource material for anyone who wants to make the Law of Attraction work for them.

So, I invite you to read this book with an open mind and heart, and to embrace the power of *Madiskarte* thinking. You'll be amazed at what you can achieve when you tap into your inner resources and align them with the universe. Enjoy the journey!

Rio Carandang

May 1, 2023

Introduction

"Madiskarte: Strategic Thinking with the Law of Attraction in Mind," is a book that combines the power of the Law of Attraction with the Filipino concept of *Madiskarte* to help you achieve your goals and dreams.

The Law of Attraction is a universal principle that states that like attracts like. In other words, our thoughts and emotions have the power to attract experiences and people that match them. The Law of Attraction has gained popularity in recent years, thanks to books like "The Secret" and "Think and Grow Rich," and the many success stories of people who have applied it in their lives.

However, as with any principle, the Law of Attraction can be misunderstood or misapplied. Some people think that all they need to do is think positive thoughts and wait for miracles to happen, while others dismiss it as pseudoscience or wishful thinking. The truth is that the Law of Attraction is a powerful tool, but it requires a strategic approach to make it work effectively.

That's where *Madiskarte* comes in. *Madiskarte* is a Filipino term that means "resourceful" or "clever." It's a trait that Filipinos are known for – the ability to find solutions and opportunities in any situation, no matter how challenging. *Madiskarte* thinking involves creativity, adaptability, and a positive attitude. It's a mindset that can enhance the Law of Attraction and make it more effective.

In this book, you'll learn how to apply the Law of Attraction in a strategic way, using *Madiskarte* thinking to create a vision, set goals, and take action towards achieving them. You'll discover the science behind the Law of Attraction, and how your thoughts and emotions can influence your experiences. You'll also learn how to overcome limiting beliefs, cultivate a positive mindset, and develop resilience and perseverance.

The book is divided into four parts. Part I provides an overview of the Law of Attraction, its basic principles, and the science behind it. Part II focuses on applying the Law of Attraction in strategic thinking, including defining your goals and dreams, creating a vision board, visualizing your success, and taking action. Part III explores different strategies for *Madiskarte* thinking, such as embracing abundance thinking, overcoming limiting beliefs, cultivating a positive mindset, practicing gratitude, and developing resilience. Part IV shows how *Madiskarte* thinking can be applied in various areas of life, such as business and entrepreneurship, career and professional development, personal relationships, and health and wellness.

This book is for anyone who wants to manifest their desires and live a fulfilling life. Whether you're a beginner or a seasoned practitioner of the Law of Attraction, you'll find new insights and practical tips in this book. The author, who has extensive experience in personal development and coaching, writes in a warm and engaging style that will motivate and inspire you.

So, get ready to embrace the power of *Madiskarte* thinking with the Law of Attraction in mind. With the right mindset and strategies, you can create the life you want and deserve. Let's get started!

What is *Madiskarte*?

Madiskarte is a concept in Filipino culture that describes a person's ability to be resourceful and clever, especially in tough situations. It's a trait that has become synonymous with Filipino culture and has been praised as a unique characteristic of Filipinos. *Madiskarte* thinking involves creativity, adaptability, and a positive attitude towards problem-solving, making it an invaluable tool for success in any area of life.

You can see *Madiskarte* in the way Filipinos navigate daily life. Whether it's finding ways to stretch a tight budget or making the most of limited resources, Filipinos have a knack for turning difficult situations to their advantage. The term itself is a combination of the Tagalog word "*diskarte*," which means strategy or tactics, and the prefix "ma," which indicates a high degree of quality or characteristic.

Madiskarte thinking is a mindset characterized by resourcefulness, creativity, and adaptability. It's a way of thinking that encourages individuals to find solutions to problems, no matter how difficult they may seem. *Madiskarte* thinking involves looking beyond conventional methods and thinking outside the box to find new and innovative solutions.

Madiskarte thinking isn't just limited to practical problem-solving. It can also be applied to personal development, such as career advancement, relationships, and achieving personal goals. By adopting a *Madiskarte* mindset, individuals can learn to overcome obstacles, overcome limiting beliefs, and create a positive and successful life.

One of the keys to *Madiskarte* thinking is having a positive attitude. A positive mindset is essential for success, as it enables individuals to focus on their goals and stay motivated, even in the face of adversity. A positive attitude can also help individuals overcome self-doubt and negative self-talk, which can often hold them back from achieving their full potential.

Another crucial aspect of *Madiskarte* thinking is adaptability. Adaptability is the ability to adjust to new situations and circumstances quickly. In today's fast-paced world, being adaptable is essential for success. By being flexible and open to new opportunities, individuals can seize opportunities and make the most of them, even if they weren't part of their original plan.

Madiskarte thinking also involves being resourceful. Resourcefulness is the ability to make the most of the resources available. Whether it's financial resources, time, or knowledge, being resourceful can help individuals achieve their goals more efficiently and effectively. By thinking creatively and finding new ways to use resources, individuals can maximize their potential and achieve their goals faster.

Madiskarte thinking is an essential tool for success in any area of life. It's a mindset characterized by creativity, adaptability, and a positive attitude towards problem-solving. By adopting a *Madiskarte* mindset, individuals can learn to overcome obstacles, overcome limiting beliefs, and create a positive and successful life. With the right mindset and strategies, anyone can develop a *Madiskarte* thinking and achieve their goals and dreams.

Why Strategic Thinking Matters

Strategic thinking is a crucial skill in today's fast-paced and ever-changing world. By analyzing the present situation, identifying potential obstacles, and coming up with creative solutions to overcome them, you can see the bigger picture and plan accordingly.

First off, strategic thinking allows you to anticipate and prepare for the future. By analyzing trends and patterns, you can identify potential challenges and opportunities before they happen. This proactive approach allows you to make informed decisions and take appropriate action to achieve your goals. With strategic thinking, you can develop a plan of action that takes into account potential obstacles and how to overcome them, increasing your chances of success.

Secondly, strategic thinking helps you prioritize your goals and allocate your resources effectively. By having a clear understanding of your objectives, you can focus your efforts and resources on what's important. Strategic thinking allows you to make informed decisions about where to invest your time, energy, and resources to achieve the greatest impact. This approach enables you to be more efficient and effective in achieving your goals.

Thirdly, strategic thinking fosters innovation and creativity. By looking at situations from different angles and perspectives, you can come up with new and innovative solutions to problems. Strategic thinking encourages you to think outside the box and challenge the status quo, leading to breakthrough ideas and approaches. By being creative and innovative, you can stay ahead of the competition and achieve your goals faster.

Fourthly, strategic thinking helps you develop a positive mindset. By anticipating challenges and potential roadblocks, you can develop a proactive mindset that enables you to face challenges with confidence and resilience. This approach helps you stay focused and motivated, even in the face of adversity. With a positive mindset, you can maintain a sense of optimism and hope, which is essential for success.

Lastly, strategic thinking helps you make informed decisions. By analyzing data and information, you can make informed decisions based on evidence rather than intuition. This approach minimizes the risk of making decisions based on emotions or biases and increases your chances of success. Strategic thinking enables you to make decisions that are well thought out and have a higher probability of achieving your desired outcome.

Strategic thinking is a vital skill that can help you achieve your goals and succeed in life. By anticipating and preparing for the future, prioritizing your goals, fostering innovation and creativity, developing a positive mindset, and making informed decisions, you can maximize your potential and achieve your desired outcomes. With strategic thinking, you can take control of your life and achieve success in any area you choose.

The Power of the Law of Attraction

The Law of Attraction is a totally awesome tool that has gained massive popularity in recent years! It's super powerful and can help you totally manifest your dreams and make them a reality. The basic idea behind it is that you attract what you focus on and believe in. So, if you focus on good vibes and positive thoughts, then you can attract totally positive experiences and opportunities into your life!

The Law of Attraction can help you overcome totally gnarly beliefs and negative thought patterns that can hold you back from reaching your full potential. By visualizing what you want and believing that you can achieve it, you can totally shift your mindset and overcome any limitations that may be holding you back!

The Law of Attraction can also help you become more stoked and happier! By focusing on positivity and gratitude, you can improve your overall well-being and increase your level of happiness. This approach can help you lead a more rad and fulfilling life, attracting more good vibes and totally awesome relationships into your life.

When you align your thoughts and emotions with your goals and aspirations, you can totally manifest the resources, opportunities, and people you need to achieve them, dude! Whether you're trying to get that sweet job or find the perfect partner, the Law of Attraction can help you make it happen. By being consistent and totally committed to the process, you can manifest your desires and create the life you've always wanted.

The Law of Attraction is an epic tool that can help you totally achieve your goals and live your dreams. By harnessing its power and combining it with strategic thinking, you can create an awesome life full of totally rad experiences, abundance, and success. So, let's get stoked and start manifesting our dreams!

Part I: Understanding the Law of Attraction

Part I of "*Madiskarte*: Strategic Thinking with the Law of Attraction in Mind" is all about understanding the Law of Attraction and how it works. This section of the book is designed to help readers gain a clear understanding of the basic principles of the Law of Attraction and how to apply them to their lives.

The Law of Attraction is a powerful force that has been around for centuries. However, in recent years it has become more popular due to the emergence of self-help gurus and motivational speakers who are spreading the word about its power.

At its core, the Law of Attraction is based on the idea that we create our own reality through our thoughts, beliefs, and emotions. This means that what we focus on and believe in, we attract into our lives. If we focus on negative thoughts and beliefs, we will attract negative experiences and outcomes. But if we focus on positive thoughts and beliefs, we will attract positive experiences and outcomes.

One of the most important aspects of the Law of Attraction is the concept of vibrational energy. This refers to the energy that we put out based on our thoughts and emotions. When we have positive thoughts and feel positive emotions, we emit a high vibrational energy that attracts positive experiences and opportunities into our lives. However, if we have negative thoughts and feel negative emotions, we emit a low vibrational energy that attracts negative experiences and outcomes.

To apply the Law of Attraction in our lives, we need to focus on our thoughts and beliefs and make sure they align with our desires and goals. This means visualizing our goals and desires and focusing on them consistently, while also eliminating negative thoughts and beliefs that may hold us back.

In addition, the Law of Attraction is all about acting towards our goals and desires. It's not enough to just think positive thoughts and visualize our goals – we also need to take consistent action towards achieving them. This means breaking down our goals into smaller, achievable steps and acting every day towards them.

In conclusion, Part I of "*Madiskarte*: Strategic Thinking with the Law of Attraction in Mind" provides readers with a comprehensive understanding of the Law of Attraction and how it works. By applying the principles of the Law of Attraction to our lives, we can create the reality we desire and achieve our goals and dreams. It's all about focusing on positive thoughts and emotions, eliminating negative thoughts and beliefs, and taking consistent action towards our goals.

The Basics of the Law of Attraction

The Law of Attraction is a universal principle that has been studied and practiced for centuries. It's a powerful force that allows us to create our own reality based on our thoughts, beliefs, and emotions. By understanding the basics of the Law of Attraction, we can learn to use this force to our advantage and achieve our goals and dreams.

The Law of Attraction is based on the principle that like attracts like. This means that our thoughts and emotions have a magnetic quality that attracts similar thoughts, emotions, and experiences into our lives. If we focus on positive thoughts and emotions, we will attract positive experiences and outcomes. On the flip side, if we focus on negative thoughts and emotions, we will attract negative experiences and outcomes.

Visualizing is a key component of the Law of Attraction. It involves creating mental images of the things we want to attract into our lives. By visualizing our desired outcomes and goals, we can create a strong emotional connection to them and increase our vibrational energy. This, in turn, makes it more likely that we will attract these things into our lives.

The Law of Attraction also emphasizes the power of affirmations. Affirmations are positive statements that we repeat to ourselves regularly to reinforce positive thoughts and beliefs. By repeating these affirmations, we can reprogram our subconscious mind to focus on positive thoughts and beliefs, which will, in turn, attract positive experiences and outcomes.

Staying in the present moment is another critical component of the Law of Attraction. This means letting go of past regrets and worries about the future and focusing on the present moment. By staying focused on the present moment, we can create a positive vibration that will attract positive experiences into our lives.

Finally, the Law of Attraction requires us to take action towards our goals and desires. Thinking positive thoughts and visualizing our goals isn't enough – we must also take consistent action towards achieving them. This means breaking down our goals into smaller, achievable steps and acting every day towards them.

The Law of Attraction is a powerful force that can be harnessed to achieve our goals and dreams. By focusing on positive thoughts and emotions, visualizing our desired outcomes and goals, using affirmations, staying present, and taking consistent action, we can create the reality we desire. The basics of the Law of Attraction are simple yet profound, and by practicing them consistently, we can experience the transformative power of this universal principle in our lives.

The Science behind the Law of Attraction

The Law of Attraction is often viewed as a mystical or spiritual concept, but there is also a scientific explanation behind its effectiveness. Understanding the science behind the Law of Attraction can help us better understand how and why it works, and how we can use it to achieve our goals and dreams.

At its core, the Law of Attraction is based on the principles of quantum physics. Quantum physics suggests that everything in the universe is made up of energy, including our thoughts, emotions, and beliefs. These energies vibrate at different frequencies, and like attracts like – which means that our thoughts and emotions can attract similar energies and experiences into our lives.

The Law of Attraction also involves the workings of our brain and the power of our subconscious mind. Our subconscious mind is responsible for our beliefs, habits, and automatic responses. It operates based on our thoughts and emotions, which means that by changing our thoughts and emotions, we can reprogram our subconscious mind and change our beliefs and habits.

Neuroplasticity is another scientific concept that supports the Law of Attraction. Neuroplasticity is the brain's ability to change and adapt throughout our lives based on our experiences and thoughts. By focusing on positive thoughts and emotions, we can create new neural pathways in our brain that reinforce positive beliefs and habits.

There is also evidence to suggest that the Law of Attraction can affect our physical body. Positive thoughts and emotions have been linked to improved immune function, lower levels of stress hormones, and increased levels of feel-good hormones such as dopamine and serotonin.

Finally, the Law of Attraction can also be explained through the concept of the reticular activating system (RAS) in our brain. The RAS is responsible for filtering out unnecessary information and bringing our attention to things that are important to us. By focusing our thoughts and emotions on our goals and desires, we can activate our RAS to bring these things to our attention and help us act towards achieving them.

In conclusion, the Law of Attraction may seem like a mystical or spiritual concept, but there is also scientific evidence to support its effectiveness. By understanding the principles of quantum physics, neuroplasticity, the power of the subconscious mind, and the workings of the RAS, we can better understand how and why the Law of Attraction works.

By practicing positive thoughts and emotions, visualizing our goals, and taking consistent action, we can use the Law of Attraction to achieve our goals and create the reality we desire. So, let's get after it! It's time to harness the power of the Law of Attraction and make our dreams a reality!

The Law of Attraction and Your Thoughts

The Law of Attraction is a seriously powerful concept that can help us achieve our goals and dreams by harnessing the power of our thoughts and beliefs. The Law of Attraction states that like attracts like, which basically means that our thoughts and beliefs can attract similar vibes and experiences into our lives.

The Law of Attraction is based on the super dope idea that our thoughts create our reality. Our thoughts and beliefs determine our perceptions, emotions, and actions. When we have positive thoughts and beliefs, we are way more likely to have lit experiences and attract positive things into our lives.

On the other hand, negative thoughts and beliefs can attract negative experiences and straight uphold us back from achieving our goals. Negative thoughts can create self-doubt, fear, and anxiety, which can prevent us from acting towards our goals.

So, it's important to be totally mindful of our thoughts and beliefs and to cultivate a positive mindset. By focusing on positive thoughts and beliefs, we can create a dope outlook on life and attract positive experiences.

One of the most powerful ways to harness the power of the Law of Attraction is through visualization. Visualization is the process of imagining yourself achieving your goals and feeling like a total boss. By visualizing your goals and desires, you are sending a clear message to the universe that you are ready to receive them.

Visualization can also help you overcome limiting beliefs and negative thoughts. When you visualize yourself achieving your goals, you are reinforcing positive beliefs and creating new neural pathways in your brain that support positive thinking and actions.

Another important aspect of the Law of Attraction and your thoughts is gratitude. Gratitude is the practice of being thankful for the blessings in your life, no matter how small they may be. By focusing on the things, you are grateful for, you are creating major good vibes and attracting even more positive experiences into your life.

The Law of Attraction and your thoughts are seriously connected. Your thoughts and beliefs create your reality, and by focusing on positive thoughts, visualizing your goals, and practicing gratitude, you can harness the power of the Law of Attraction to achieve your goals and create the life you totally want. So, let's embrace positivity and the power of our thoughts! It's time to manifest our dreams and live our best lives.

The Law of Attraction and Your Emotions

The Law of Attraction and your emotions go hand in hand, folks. It's a powerful concept that involves attracting similar vibes and experiences into your life through your thoughts and beliefs. But did y'all know that your emotions play a major role in manifesting your desires through the Law of Attraction?

Your emotions create vibrations that the universe picks up on. When you're feeling good, happy, and grateful, you're sending out high vibes that attract positive experiences into your life. On the other hand, when you're feeling down, fearful, or angry, you're sending out low vibes that can attract negative experiences into your life. It's a vicious cycle, folks!

That's why it's so important to manage your emotions and cultivate positive feelings as much as possible. One of the best ways to do this is through mindfulness and meditation. By practicing mindfulness and meditation, you can become more aware of your emotions and learn to manage them in a positive way.

Another critical aspect of the Law of Attraction and your emotions is the concept of emotional resonance. This means that your emotions can resonate with the emotions of others, attracting similar experiences into your life. So, if you're feeling constantly angry or anxious, you may attract people and situations that reflect those emotions.

To avoid this, it's essential to cultivate positive emotions and surround yourself with positive people and experiences. This can help you attract even more positivity into your life and manifest your desires more easily.

Lastly, gratitude is a super powerful emotion that can help you manifest your desires through the Law of

Attraction. When you feel grateful for the blessings in your life, you're sending out high vibes that attract even more blessings into your life. Gratitude can also help you overcome negative emotions and limiting beliefs that may be holding you back from achieving your goals.

The Law of Attraction and your emotions are seriously connected, y'all. By being mindful of your emotions, cultivating positivity, and embracing gratitude, you can manifest your dreams and live your best life. So, let's get to it!

Part II: Applying the Law of Attraction in Strategic Thinking

"*Madiskarte*: Strategic Thinking with the Law of Attraction in Mind" is where the rubber meets the road, folks. In this section of the book, we explore how to apply the Law of Attraction in strategic thinking to manifest our desires.

Strategic thinking is all about creating a plan of action and executing it with purpose and intention. When you combine strategic thinking with the Law of Attraction, you can create a powerful manifestation machine that attracts your desires into your life.

The first step in applying the Law of Attraction in strategic thinking is to set clear and specific goals. You need to know exactly what you want to manifest in your life, and you need to be able to visualize it in great detail. The Law of Attraction responds to clear intentions and vivid imagery, so the more specific you can be about your desires, the better.

The next step is to focus on the feeling of already having achieved your goals. This is where the Law of Attraction really comes into play, folks. By visualizing yourself already having achieved your goals and feeling the emotions that come with that achievement, you can attract those experiences into your life. The Law of Attraction responds to emotions, so it's crucial to focus on feeling good and positive about your desires.

Another critical aspect of applying the Law of Attraction in strategic thinking is to take inspired action. This means taking action that is aligned with your goals and feels good to you. When you act from a place of inspiration and alignment, you're sending out high vibes that attract even more positivity into your life.

It's also important to be open and receptive to opportunities that come your way. The Law of Attraction works in mysterious ways, and sometimes the universe will present you with unexpected opportunities that align with your desires. By being open and receptive to these opportunities, you can manifest your desires more easily.

Finally, gratitude is a critical component of applying the Law of Attraction in strategic thinking. By feeling grateful for the progress, you've made towards your goals and the blessings in your life, you're sending out high vibes that attract even more positivity into your life. Gratitude also helps you stay focused on the positive aspects of your life and can help you overcome any obstacles or challenges that may arise.

In conclusion, Part II of "*Madiskarte*: Strategic Thinking with the Law of Attraction in Mind" is all about applying the Law of Attraction in strategic thinking to manifest your desires and achieve your goals. By setting clear goals, focusing on positive emotions, taking inspired action, being open to opportunities, and embracing gratitude, you can create a powerful manifestation machine that attracts the life you truly desire. So let's get to it, folks! Part II: Applying the Law of Attraction in Strategic Thinking

"*Madiskarte*: Strategic Thinking with the Law of Attraction in Mind" is where the rubber meets the road, folks. In this section of the book, we explore how to apply the Law of Attraction in strategic thinking to manifest our desires.

Strategic thinking is all about creating a plan of action and executing it with purpose and intention. When you combine strategic thinking with the Law of

Attraction, you can create a powerful manifestation machine that attracts your desires into your life.

The first step in applying the Law of Attraction in strategic thinking is to set clear and specific goals. You need to know exactly what you want to manifest in your life, and you need to be able to visualize it in detail. The Law of Attraction responds to clear intentions and vivid imagery, so the more specific you can be about your desires, the better.

The next step is to focus on the feeling of already having achieved your goals. This is where the Law of Attraction really comes into play, folks. By visualizing yourself already having achieved your goals and feeling the emotions that come with that achievement, you can attract those experiences into your life. The Law of Attraction responds to emotions, so it's crucial to focus on feeling good and positive about your desires.

Another critical aspect of applying the Law of Attraction in strategic thinking is to take inspired action. This means taking action that is aligned with your goals and feels good to you. When you act from a place of inspiration and alignment, you're sending out high vibes that attract even more positivity into your life.

It's also important to be open and receptive to opportunities that come your way. The Law of Attraction works in mysterious ways, and sometimes the universe will present you with unexpected opportunities that align with your desires. By being open and receptive to these opportunities, you can manifest your desires more easily.

Finally, gratitude is a critical component of applying the Law of Attraction in strategic thinking. By feeling grateful for the progress, you've made towards your goals and the blessings in your life, you're sending out high vibes that attract even more positivity into your life. Gratitude also helps you stay focused on the positive aspects of your life and can help you overcome any obstacles or challenges that may arise.

Part II of "*Madiskarte*: Strategic Thinking with the Law of Attraction in Mind" is all about applying the Law of Attraction in strategic thinking to manifest your desires and achieve your goals. By setting clear goals, focusing on positive emotions, taking inspired action, being open to opportunities, and embracing gratitude, you can create a powerful manifestation machine that attracts the life you truly desire. So, let's get to it, folks!

Defining Your Goals and Dreams

When it comes to applying the law of attraction in strategic thinking, it is crucial to start by defining your goals and dreams. This process helps you to focus your energy and attention on what you want to achieve and attract into your life.

One of the key principles of the law of attraction is that your thoughts and emotions create your reality. Therefore, it is essential to have a clear understanding of what you want to create in your life. Defining your goals and dreams helps you to get clarity on what you want to attract and manifest.

To define your goals and dreams, start by asking yourself some questions. What do you want to achieve in your personal and professional life? What kind of relationships do you want to have? What kind of lifestyle do you want to lead? Write down your answers and be as specific as possible.

Once you have a clear understanding of your goals and dreams, create a vision board or visual representation of your desires. This process helps to create a clear image in your mind of what you want to attract and serves as a powerful reminder of your aspirations.

It is important to remember that your goals and dreams should be aligned with your values and beliefs. They should also be realistic and achievable. Setting unrealistic goals can lead to disappointment and frustration, which can negatively impact your thoughts and emotions, and ultimately, your ability to attract what you desire.

Another crucial aspect of defining your goals and dreams is to focus on the present moment. While it is essential to have a clear vision of your future, it is equally important to be mindful and present in the current moment. Enjoy the journey towards achieving your goals and dreams, and don't let your focus on the future detract from the present.

Defining your goals and dreams is the first step towards applying the law of attraction in strategic thinking. By clarifying your desires, creating a visual representation of your aspirations, and staying aligned with your values and beliefs, you can focus your energy and attention on attracting what you want in life. Remember to stay present in the moment and enjoy the journey towards achieving your goals and dreams.

Creating a Vision Board for Your Goals

Visualizing your goals and dreams is an important step in manifesting them into reality. One powerful tool to help you visualize your goals is creating a vision board. A vision board is a collage of images, quotes, and affirmations that represent your goals and aspirations. The act of creating a vision board helps you clarify your intentions, stay focused on your goals, and attract the resources and opportunities needed to achieve them.

To create a vision board, start by thinking about your goals and what you want to manifest in your life. This can include personal goals such as health, relationships, and personal growth, as well as professional goals such as career advancement or starting your own business. Once you have a clear idea of your goals, gather images and words that represent them. This can include photos from magazines, quotes, affirmations, and even personal photos or mementos.

Next, find a large piece of poster board or a corkboard to use as the base for your vision board. Use glue or tape to attach your images and words to the board, arranging them in a way that feels meaningful and inspiring to you. You can also add decorations such as stickers, markers, or glitter to make your vision board more personal and creative.

Once your vision board is complete, place it in a prominent location where you will see it every day. This can be in your bedroom, office, or any other space where you spend a lot of time. Spend a few minutes each day looking at your vision board and visualizing yourself achieving your goals. Imagine how it will feel to have achieved your goals and allow yourself to feel the emotions associated with that achievement.

By creating a vision board, you are engaging in the process of visualization, which is a powerful tool for manifesting your desires. When you focus your thoughts and emotions on your goals, you send a signal to the universe that you are ready and willing to receive the resources and opportunities needed to achieve them. The Law of Attraction states that like attracts like, so by focusing on the positive aspects of your goals, you will attract more positive experiences and opportunities into your life.

In addition to visualizing your goals, acting is also an important part of manifesting them into reality. Use your vision board as a guide to help you make decisions and take actions that align with your goals. For example, if one of your goals is to start a business, use your vision board to brainstorm ideas and create a plan of action.

In summary, creating a vision board is a powerful tool for manifesting your goals and dreams. By visualizing your goals and focusing on the positive aspects of achieving them, you can attract the resources and opportunities needed to make them a reality. Use your vision board as a guide to help you take action and make decisions that align with your goals. Remember, the Law of Attraction responds to your thoughts and emotions, so stay focused on your goals and believe that they are possible. Creating a Vision Board for Your Goals

Visualizing your goals and dreams is an important step in manifesting them into reality. One powerful tool to help you visualize your goals is creating a vision board. A vision board is a collage of images, quotes, and affirmations that represent your goals and aspirations. The act of creating a vision board helps you clarify your intentions, stay focused on your goals, and attract the resources and opportunities needed to achieve them.

To create a vision board, start by thinking about your goals and what you want to manifest in your life. This can include personal goals such as health, relationships, and personal growth, as well as professional goals such as career advancement or starting your own business. Once you have a clear idea of your goals, gather images and words that represent them. This can include photos from magazines, quotes, affirmations, and even personal photos or mementos.

Next, find a large piece of poster board or a corkboard to use as the base for your vision board. Use glue or tape to attach your images and words to the board, arranging them in a way that feels meaningful and inspiring to you. You can also add decorations such as stickers, markers, or glitter to make your vision board more personal and creative.

Once your vision board is complete, place it in a prominent location where you will see it every day. This can be in your bedroom, office, or any other space where you spend a lot of time. Spend a few minutes each day looking at your vision board and visualizing yourself achieving your goals. Imagine how it will feel to have achieved your goals and allow yourself to feel the emotions associated with that achievement.

By creating a vision board, you are engaging in the process of visualization, which is a powerful tool for manifesting your desires. When you focus your thoughts and emotions on your goals, you send a signal to the universe that you are ready and willing to receive the resources and opportunities needed to achieve them. The Law of Attraction states that like attracts like, so by focusing on the positive aspects of your goals, you will attract more positive experiences and opportunities into your life.

In addition to visualizing your goals, taking action is also an important part of manifesting them into reality. Use your vision board as a guide to help you make decisions and take actions that align with your goals. For example, if one of your goals is to start a business, use your vision board to brainstorm ideas and create a plan of action.

In summary, creating a vision board is a powerful tool for manifesting your goals and dreams. By visualizing your goals and focusing on the positive aspects of achieving them, you can attract the resources and opportunities needed to make them a reality. Use your vision board as a guide to help you act and make decisions that align with your goals. Remember, the Law of Attraction responds to your thoughts and emotions, so stay focused on your goals and believe that they are possible.

Visualizing Your Success

Visualization is a powerful tool that can help individuals achieve their goals and manifest their dreams. In the context of the Law of Attraction, visualization is an essential practice that helps individuals focus on their desires and create a positive mindset that attracts success.

To visualize your success, you need to first define your goals and dreams. This means being specific about what you want to achieve, and why it is important to you. Once you have clarity on your goals, you can begin to create a mental image of yourself achieving them. This mental image should be as vivid and detailed as possible, including sensory details like the sights, sounds, and emotions associated with achieving your goals.

When you visualize your success, it is important to do so with a sense of belief and confidence. You need to truly believe that you can achieve your goals and that the universe is working in your favor to make it happen. This sense of belief and confidence can be strengthened through regular meditation and affirmations, which help to reprogram your subconscious mind and overcome any limiting beliefs that may be holding you back.

It is also important to visualize your success in a positive and grateful manner. Instead of focusing on what you don't have or what you haven't achieved yet, focus on the abundance and blessings in your life. This positive mindset will help to attract even more positive energy and opportunities into your life.

One powerful technique for visualizing your success is to create a mental movie. This involves imagining yourself in a movie theater, watching a movie of your life as if it has already happened. This mental movie should be filled with positive and empowering scenes of you achieving your goals and living your dreams. As you watch this mental movie, feel the emotions associated with achieving your goals, and allow yourself to experience the joy and excitement of success.

Visualization is a practice that can be done at anytime, anywhere. Whether you do it in the morning before starting your day, or before going to bed at night, the key is to make it a regular part of your routine. With consistent practice, you will begin to notice that the universe responds to your positive energy and that you are able to manifest your desires with greater ease and speed.

Visualization is a powerful technique that can help you to achieve your goals and manifest your dreams. By focusing on your goals with a sense of belief and confidence, and visualizing yourself achieving them with positivity and gratitude, you can attract success and abundance into your life. With regular practice, you can harness the power of the Law of Attraction to create the life you desire.

Taking Action with the Law of Attraction

The Law of Attraction is a powerful tool for achieving your goals and creating the life you desire, but it is not enough to simply visualize and believe that you will receive what you want. Taking action is an essential part of the process. In fact, action is what turns your dreams into reality.

Taking action with the Law of Attraction means that you are actively working towards your goals while maintaining a positive mindset and belief in your ability to achieve them. This means that you are taking steps to move closer to your desired outcome, even if you do not know exactly how you will get there.

One of the keys to taking action with the Law of Attraction is to focus on the present moment. This means that you are fully engaged in the tasks and activities that will help you achieve your goals, without getting distracted by past failures or future doubts.

Another important aspect of taking action with the Law of Attraction is to maintain a positive attitude and belief in yourself. This means that you do not allow negative thoughts or self-doubt to hold you back, but instead, you focus on your strengths and your ability to succeed.

Taking action with the Law of Attraction also means that you are willing to take risks and step outside of your comfort zone. This may mean trying new things or pursuing opportunities that you may have been afraid of in the past.

It is important to remember that taking action with the Law of Attraction does not guarantee immediate success. However, it does increase the likelihood that you will achieve your goals over time. This is because taking action creates momentum and attracts opportunities that will help you reach your desired outcome.

In order to take action with the Law of Attraction, it is important to create a plan and set specific goals that are aligned with your vision and values. This plan should include actionable steps that will move you closer to your goals, as well as a timeline for when you would like to achieve them.

Once you have created a plan, it is important to take consistent action towards your goals, even if it is just small steps each day. This will help you build momentum and maintain a positive mindset as you work towards your desired outcome.

Taking action with the Law of Attraction is an essential part of achieving your goals and creating the life you desire. By maintaining a positive mindset, focusing on the present moment, and taking risks, you can attract opportunities and create the momentum needed to make your dreams a reality.

Part III: Strategies for *Madiskarte* Thinking

Part III of the book "*Madiskarte*: Strategic Thinking with the Law of Attraction in Mind" covers different strategies to help readers apply the concepts of the Law of Attraction in their daily lives. By implementing these strategies, readers can improve their mindset, attract positive experiences, and achieve their goals.

The first strategy covered in this section is mindfulness. Mindfulness is the practice of being present and fully engaged in the present moment, without judgment. It is a powerful tool that can help individuals improve their mental and emotional well-being. By being mindful, individuals can focus their attention on positive thoughts and experiences, which can help attract more positive experiences in the future.

Another strategy covered in this section is the power of positive affirmations. Positive affirmations are statements that individuals repeat to themselves to promote positive thinking and self-talk. By repeating positive affirmations, individuals can reprogram their subconscious mind to focus on positive experiences and outcomes.

The next strategy covered in this section is the importance of gratitude. Gratitude is the practice of focusing on and appreciating the good things in one's life. By focusing on gratitude, individuals can shift their mindset to a more positive and optimistic one, which can help attract more positive experiences.

The final strategy covered in this section is the power of manifestation. Manifestation is the process of visualizing and creating what one wants in life through the power of their thoughts and beliefs. By aligning one's thoughts, beliefs, and actions with their desired outcome, individuals can manifest their dreams and goals into reality.

Part III of "*Madiskarte*: Strategic Thinking with the Law of Attraction in Mind" covers various strategies that readers can use to apply the Law of Attraction in their daily lives. By incorporating these strategies into their daily routine, readers can shift their mindset to a more positive and optimistic one, which can help attract more positive experiences and achieve their goals.

Embracing Abundance Thinking

Abundance thinking is a powerful strategy that can help you achieve your goals and manifest your dreams. At its core, abundance thinking is the belief that there is enough of everything in the universe to go around. It's about adopting a mindset of abundance and prosperity, rather than one of scarcity and lack. By embracing abundance thinking, you can attract more positivity and abundance into your life, which in turn can help you achieve success and live a happier, more fulfilling life.

To start embracing abundance thinking, it's important to first recognize any limiting beliefs you may have around scarcity and lack. These limiting beliefs can hold you back from achieving your goals and manifesting your dreams. Some common limiting beliefs include:

"I'll never have enough money."

"There aren't enough opportunities out there for me."

"I'm not talented enough to succeed."

By identifying these limiting beliefs, you can start to challenge and replace them with more empowering, abundance-based beliefs. For example:

"There is always enough money for what I need."

"There are endless opportunities available to me."

"I have unique talents and abilities that make me successful."

Once you've identified and replaced your limiting beliefs, you can start taking action towards manifesting abundance in your life. One effective strategy is to practice gratitude regularly. By focusing on what you're grateful for, you attract more positivity and abundance into your life. Make a habit of writing down three things you're grateful for each day, and reflect on them regularly.

Another strategy is to surround yourself with positive, supportive people who share your abundance mindset. Seek out mentors and role models who have achieved success in areas that you're interested in, and learn from their experiences. Connect with like-minded individuals who can support and encourage you on your journey towards abundance and success.

It's also important to take action towards your goals, rather than just visualizing or wishing for them. The law of attraction works best when combined with action, so make sure you're taking steps towards manifesting your dreams. This could include networking, seeking out new opportunities, or investing in your own personal growth and development.

Overall, embracing abundance thinking is a powerful strategy that can help you achieve success and manifest your dreams. By challenging limiting beliefs, practicing gratitude, surrounding yourself with positivity, and taking action towards your goals, you can start attracting abundance and prosperity into your life.

Overcoming Limiting Beliefs

Limiting beliefs can be a major roadblock to achieving your goals and dreams. These beliefs are often formed early in life based on our experiences and interactions with others. They are deeply ingrained and can affect how we think, feel, and act in our daily lives. The good news is that it is possible to overcome these limiting beliefs and adopt a more positive mindset through the practice of *Madiskarte* thinking.

One common limiting belief is the belief that we are not good enough. This belief can manifest itself in different ways, such as self-doubt, procrastination, and fear of failure. To overcome this limiting belief, it is important to recognize and challenge it. Ask yourself, "Is this belief really true? What evidence do I have to support it?" By questioning the validity of the belief, you can begin to see it for what it is - a self-imposed barrier that is holding you back.

Another limiting belief is the belief that success is only for the lucky few. This belief can lead to a defeatist attitude and a lack of motivation to take action towards your goals. To overcome this belief, it is important to recognize that success is not a matter of luck, but of hard work, perseverance, and strategic thinking. By adopting a *Madiskarte* mindset and taking deliberate steps towards your goals, you can increase your chances of success.

A third limiting belief is the belief that we are not worthy of success or happiness. This belief can stem from past experiences of rejection or failure, or from messages received from others. To overcome this limiting belief, it is important to practice self-compassion and self-care. Acknowledge your strengths and achievements and treat yourself with kindness and respect. By practicing self-love and self-acceptance, you can begin to see yourself as deserving of success and happiness.

One effective strategy for overcoming limiting beliefs is the use of affirmations. Affirmations are positive statements that reflect the reality you want to create for yourself. By repeating these statements daily, you can reprogram your subconscious mind and replace negative beliefs with positive ones. Examples of affirmations include "I am capable of achieving my goals," "I deserve success and happiness," and "I am worthy of love and respect."

In addition to affirmations, visualization is another powerful tool for overcoming limiting beliefs. Visualization involves creating mental images of yourself achieving your goals and experiencing the emotions associated with that achievement. By vividly imagining your success, you can create a sense of confidence and motivation that will help you overcome any limiting beliefs that may be holding you back.

Overcoming limiting beliefs is essential to achieving success and living a fulfilling life. By adopting a *Madiskarte* mindset and practicing strategies such as affirmations and visualization, you can break free from self-imposed barriers and realize your full potential. Remember that your beliefs shape your reality, so choose beliefs that empower you and lead you towards the life you want to live.

Cultivating a Positive Mindset

In the pursuit of achieving our goals and dreams, cultivating a positive mindset is crucial. It is a mindset that enables us to navigate through challenges and setbacks, keep our focus on the opportunities and possibilities, and maintain a strong belief in ourselves and our abilities. Cultivating a positive mindset can be challenging, especially when we are facing difficult circumstances, but it is not impossible.

One of the first steps to cultivating a positive mindset is to practice gratitude. This means acknowledging and appreciating the good things in our lives, regardless of how small they may be. It could be something as simple as having a roof over our heads, good health, or supportive relationships. By focusing on the positive aspects of our lives, we train our minds to look for the good in every situation.

Another important aspect of cultivating a positive mindset is to surround ourselves with positive influences. This could mean spending time with people who uplift us and inspire us, reading books and articles that motivate us, or listening to podcasts and audiobooks that help us stay focused and optimistic. It is also important to limit exposure to negative influences such as toxic people or negative news.

In addition to gratitude and positive influences, practicing positive self-talk is also crucial in cultivating a positive mindset. We often talk to ourselves in ways that we would never talk to someone else, and this negative self-talk can limit our potential and derail our progress. By consciously choosing to speak to ourselves in positive and empowering ways, we can change our internal dialogue and increase our confidence and self-belief.

It is important to note that cultivating a positive mindset does not mean ignoring or denying the challenges and difficulties we face. Rather, it means acknowledging them, but choosing to approach them with a positive attitude and a belief that we have the ability to overcome them.

Finally, it is important to remember that cultivating a positive mindset is an ongoing process that requires consistent effort and practice. It is not a one-time fix or a quick solution, but a lifelong journey. By consistently choosing to focus on the positive, surround ourselves with positivity, and speak to ourselves positively, we can develop a resilient and optimistic mindset that will serve us well in achieving our goals and dreams.

Cultivating a positive mindset is an essential aspect of strategic thinking and achieving success. By practicing gratitude, surrounding ourselves with positive influences, practicing positive self-talk, and embracing challenges with a positive attitude, we can develop a mindset that is strong, resilient, and capable of achieving our dreams.

Practicing Gratitude and Appreciation

Gratitude and appreciation are powerful tools that can help us cultivate a positive mindset and attract more abundance into our lives. In the context of *Madiskarte* thinking, the practice of gratitude and appreciation can be a key strategy for harnessing the Law of Attraction to achieve our goals and dreams.

Gratitude is the act of acknowledging and appreciating the positive aspects of our lives. It can be as simple as taking a few moments each day to reflect on the things we are grateful for, such as our health, our relationships, our home, our job, or the opportunities that come our way. When we focus on what we have rather than what we lack, we create a positive mindset that attracts more positivity into our lives.

Appreciation goes a step further than gratitude by actively expressing our gratitude to others. It involves acknowledging the good qualities and actions of the people around us and letting them know that we value them. This can be as simple as saying thank you or giving a compliment, but it can have a profound impact on our relationships and our overall sense of well-being.

In the context of the Law of Attraction, gratitude and appreciation work by creating a positive energetic vibration that attracts more positivity into our lives. When we focus on the good in our lives, we signal to the universe that we are open to receiving more of it. This can manifest in many different ways, such as new opportunities, increased abundance, or improved relationships.

To practice gratitude and appreciation, it can be helpful to establish a daily practice. This might involve setting aside a few minutes each morning or evening to reflect on the things you are grateful for or to express your appreciation to others. You might also consider keeping a gratitude journal where you write down the things you are grateful for each day.

Another powerful strategy for practicing gratitude and appreciation is to focus on the positive aspects of challenging situations. When we face difficulties or setbacks, it can be easy to get caught up in negative thinking and lose sight of the good that is present. By shifting our focus to the positive aspects of the situation, we can cultivate a sense of gratitude and appreciation even in the face of adversity.

Practicing gratitude and appreciation is a powerful strategy for cultivating a positive mindset and harnessing the Law of Attraction to achieve our goals and dreams. By focusing on the good in our lives and expressing our appreciation to others, we create a positive energetic vibration that attracts more positivity into our lives. As we cultivate a sense of gratitude and appreciation, we become more open to the abundance and opportunities that surround us, and we are better able to manifest our desires and live the life we truly desire.

Developing Resilience and Perseverance

Developing Resilience and Perseverance are important factors in achieving success in life. This is especially true when it comes to applying the Law of Attraction. In the book "*Madiskarte*: Strategic Thinking with the Law of Attraction in Mind," the author emphasizes the importance of resilience and perseverance in the manifestation of one's desires.

Resilience refers to the ability to adapt to difficult situations, bounce back from setbacks, and maintain a positive attitude in the face of adversity. It is a crucial skill to develop when pursuing one's goals, as obstacles and challenges are inevitable. Without resilience, it can be easy to give up or become discouraged when faced with setbacks. However, those who are resilient are better equipped to face challenges and continue to move forward.

Perseverance is another important factor in achieving success. It refers to the ability to persist in the face of difficulty and to continue working towards a goal, even when progress is slow, or setbacks occur. Perseverance is often the key to success, as many successful individuals have faced numerous failures before finally achieving their goals.

So how can one develop resilience and perseverance? One way is to practice a growth mindset, which involves viewing setbacks and failures as opportunities for growth and learning. Instead of seeing setbacks as a sign of failure, a growth mindset allows individuals to view them as opportunities to learn and improve.

Another important aspect of developing resilience and perseverance is to maintain a positive attitude. Positive thinking can help individuals maintain a sense of hope and optimism, even in difficult situations. This can help them stay motivated and focused on their goals, even when faced with challenges.

Finally, it is important to have a support system in place. Surrounding oneself with positive and supportive individuals can help provide encouragement and motivation during difficult times. It can also be helpful to seek out mentors or role models who have successfully achieved similar goals, as they can provide valuable guidance and advice.

In summary, developing resilience and perseverance are crucial aspects of achieving success in life and applying the Law of Attraction. By cultivating a growth mindset, maintaining a positive attitude, and seeking out a support system, individuals can better equip themselves to overcome challenges and persist in pursuing their goals.

Part IV: *Madiskarte* Thinking in Action

"*Madiskarte*: Strategic Thinking with the Law of Attraction in Mind" is a book that focuses on the power of the Law of Attraction and how it can be applied to strategic thinking in order to achieve one's goals and dreams. Part IV of the book is titled "*Madiskarte* Thinking in Action" and it is where the theories and strategies discussed in the previous sections are put into practice. This section of the book focuses on case studies and real-life examples of people who have successfully used the *Madiskarte* approach to achieve their goals.

The first chapter of this section focuses on the importance of taking action. The Law of Attraction alone is not enough to achieve one's goals. Action is necessary to bring those goals into reality. The chapter discusses the different types of action that are necessary for success, including taking small steps, being persistent, and learning from mistakes. It also discusses the importance of having a plan and being flexible enough to make adjustments when necessary.

The second chapter focuses on the role of visualization in achieving success. The Law of Attraction teaches us that our thoughts and emotions have the power to shape our reality. Visualization is a powerful tool that can help us to focus our thoughts and emotions on the outcomes that we want to achieve. The chapter provides practical tips for using visualization effectively, such as using all of your senses, making your visualizations vivid and specific, and practicing regularly.

The third chapter of Part IV focuses on overcoming limiting beliefs. Limiting beliefs are the negative thoughts and beliefs that hold us back from achieving our goals. The chapter provides strategies for identifying and overcoming limiting beliefs, such as reframing negative thoughts into positive ones and using affirmations to reprogram the subconscious mind.

The fourth chapter focuses on the importance of cultivating a positive mindset. A positive mindset is essential for success because it helps us to stay motivated, focused, and resilient in the face of challenges. The chapter discusses the benefits of positive thinking and provides strategies for cultivating a positive mindset, such as focusing on gratitude, practicing mindfulness, and surrounding oneself with positive influences.

The final chapter of Part IV focuses on the importance of developing resilience and perseverance. Resilience and perseverance are necessary for success because they help us to bounce back from setbacks and keep moving forward towards our goals. The chapter provides practical strategies for developing resilience and perseverance, such as learning from failures, taking calculated risks, and seeking out support from others.

Overall, Part IV of "*Madiskarte*: Strategic Thinking with the Law of Attraction in Mind" provides practical advice and strategies for putting the *Madiskarte* approach into practice. The case studies and real-life examples provide inspiration and motivation for readers to apply the principles of the Law of Attraction to their own lives. By taking action, visualizing success, overcoming limiting beliefs, cultivating a positive mindset, and developing resilience and perseverance, readers can achieve their goals and live the life they desire.

Madiskarte in Business and Entrepreneurship

Madiskarte thinking, with its focus on strategic thinking and the Law of Attraction, can be a valuable tool in the world of business and entrepreneurship. By using the principles of *Madiskarte*, entrepreneurs and business owners can better visualize and achieve their goals, overcome limiting beliefs, and cultivate a positive mindset that leads to success.

One key aspect of *Madiskarte* thinking in business is goal-setting. By defining specific, achievable goals, entrepreneurs can create a clear path to success. This involves not only defining goals but also creating a plan of action to achieve those goals. Visualizing success and creating a vision board can help entrepreneurs stay focused and motivated as they work towards their goals.

Another important aspect of *Madiskarte* thinking in business is overcoming limiting beliefs. Many entrepreneurs struggle with self-doubt and negative thoughts that can hold them back. By using *Madiskarte* principles such as gratitude, positive thinking, and resilience, entrepreneurs can overcome these limiting beliefs and move towards success.

Cultivating a positive mindset is also essential in business. Entrepreneurs face numerous challenges and setbacks along the way, and a positive mindset can help them stay focused and motivated. This involves focusing on the positive aspects of the business and cultivating an attitude of gratitude and appreciation.

Practicing *Madiskarte* thinking can also help entrepreneurs make better decisions. By using visualization and the Law of Attraction, entrepreneurs can attract the right opportunities and make choices that align with their goals and values.

In addition, *Madiskarte* thinking can be especially helpful in the realm of networking and relationship building. Entrepreneurs can use visualization and the Law of Attraction to attract the right people and opportunities, and cultivate positive relationships with clients, partners, and collaborators.

Overall, *Madiskarte* thinking can be a powerful tool for entrepreneurs and business owners looking to achieve success. By focusing on strategic thinking, visualization, and the Law of Attraction, entrepreneurs can overcome limiting beliefs, cultivate a positive mindset, and achieve their goals in the world of business and entrepreneurship.

Madiskarte in Career and Professional Development

In today's fast-paced world, career and professional development have become essential for success. The job market is more competitive than ever, and it takes more than just hard work to advance your career. This is where *Madiskarte* thinking comes in. *Madiskarte* is a Filipino term that means strategic thinking, and it is a mindset that can help you achieve your career goals by combining the principles of the Law of Attraction with strategic thinking.

The Law of Attraction states that we attract what we focus on. In other words, our thoughts and emotions influence the outcomes we experience in our lives. By adopting a *Madiskarte* mindset in our careers, we can leverage the power of the Law of Attraction to achieve success.

The first step to adopting a *Madiskarte* mindset in your career is to define your goals. What do you want to achieve in your career? Do you want to climb the corporate ladder, start your own business, or switch careers? Once you have defined your goals, you can start visualizing your success. Visualization is a powerful tool that can help you attract the opportunities and resources you need to achieve your goals.

Another important aspect of *Madiskarte* thinking in career development is networking. The people you know and the relationships you build can play a crucial role in your success. By cultivating positive relationships with colleagues, industry leaders, and mentors, you can open doors to new opportunities and gain valuable insights and advice.

In addition to networking, continuous learning and development are also essential for *Madiskarte* thinking in career development. The job market is constantly evolving, and it is essential to stay up-to-date with the latest trends and technologies in your field. By investing in your education and professional development, you can stay ahead of the curve and position yourself for success.

Another aspect of *Madiskarte* thinking in career development is taking calculated risks. Starting a new business or taking on a new job opportunity can be daunting, but it can also be an opportunity for growth and advancement. By taking calculated risks, you can step outside of your comfort zone and discover new opportunities for success.

Lastly, cultivating a positive mindset is crucial for *Madiskarte* thinking in career development. It is important to focus on your strengths, acknowledge your weaknesses, and maintain a positive attitude even in the face of challenges. By maintaining a positive attitude, you can attract positive outcomes and overcome obstacles that may stand in the way of your success.

Madiskarte thinking can be a powerful tool for career and professional development. By combining the principles of the Law of Attraction with strategic thinking, you can define your goals, visualize your success, build positive relationships, invest in your education and professional development, take calculated risks, and maintain a positive mindset. With these tools at your disposal, you can achieve your career goals and position yourself for long-term success.

Madiskarte in Personal Relationships

Madiskarte is a powerful tool that can be used to enhance various aspects of life, including personal relationships. The Law of Attraction can help us to attract positive and fulfilling relationships, whether it be romantic or platonic. By using *Madiskarte* thinking in personal relationships, we can learn to develop meaningful connections with others and create a positive and fulfilling life.

The first step to using *Madiskarte* thinking in personal relationships is to focus on our own thoughts and emotions. We must learn to be positive and optimistic in our own lives, as this will help us to attract positive people and experiences into our lives. This means that we must work to develop a positive mindset, focusing on our strengths and the positive aspects of our lives, and avoiding negative self-talk and self-doubt.

Another important aspect of *Madiskarte* in personal relationships is the importance of setting clear intentions and goals. We must be clear about what we want in a relationship, and we must be willing to put in the work necessary to achieve those goals. This may involve taking steps to improve our communication skills, practicing active listening, and being open and honest with ourselves and others.

It is also important to remember that relationships are a two-way street. We must be willing to give as well as receive, and we must be open to the needs and wants of others. By practicing empathy and understanding, we can develop deeper and more meaningful connections with the people in our lives.

In addition to focusing on our own thoughts and emotions, setting clear intentions and goals, and practicing empathy and understanding, *Madiskarte* thinking can also help us to overcome obstacles in our personal relationships. This may involve learning to communicate effectively, setting healthy boundaries, and practicing forgiveness and acceptance.

Finally, *Madiskarte* thinking can help us to cultivate gratitude and appreciation in our personal relationships. By focusing on the positive aspects of our relationships, we can develop a deeper sense of gratitude and appreciation for the people in our lives, which can in turn strengthen our connections and create a more fulfilling life.

In conclusion, *Madiskarte* thinking can be a powerful tool for enhancing personal relationships. By focusing on our own thoughts and emotions, setting clear intentions and goals, practicing empathy and understanding, overcoming obstacles, and cultivating gratitude and appreciation, we can create deeper and more meaningful connections with the people in our lives.

Madiskarte in Health and Wellness

Madiskarte, a Filipino term for strategic thinking or being resourceful, can also be applied to health and wellness. The Law of Attraction, a principle that states that like attracts like, can be utilized to achieve optimal health and wellness. By applying *Madiskarte* thinking, one can create a positive and healthy environment for the mind and body.

One of the fundamental aspects of *Madiskarte* thinking in health and wellness is setting clear and specific health goals. The Law of Attraction works by focusing on the positive outcome and energy that a person wants to attract. Therefore, by setting clear and specific health goals, an individual can focus their energy and attention on achieving those goals. For example, if a person wants to lose weight, they should set a specific goal, such as losing 10 pounds in two months. This will help them stay motivated and focused on their objective.

Visualization is another important technique that can be used in *Madiskarte* thinking for health and wellness. Visualization is the process of imagining oneself in a particular situation, which helps the brain to create a positive image of that situation. By visualizing oneself as healthy, happy, and vibrant, the brain can create positive neural pathways that can lead to actual physical changes in the body. This technique can be used to overcome obstacles, reduce stress, and increase motivation.

Gratitude is also an essential component of *Madiskarte* thinking in health and wellness. Gratitude is the act of recognizing and appreciating the positive aspects of life. By focusing on the good things, an individual can create positive energy and attract more positive experiences. Practicing gratitude can also reduce stress, boost the immune system, and improve mental health.

In addition, *Madiskarte* thinking can also be applied to nutrition and exercise. By being resourceful and creative, one can find healthy and enjoyable ways to nourish and move their body. For example, instead of relying on fast food for convenience, a person can prepare healthy meals in advance and bring them to work. Or, instead of feeling obligated to go to the gym, a person can find physical activities they enjoy, such as hiking, dancing, or swimming.

Finally, *Madiskarte* thinking in health and wellness also involves taking responsibility for one's own health. This means being aware of one's body and taking proactive steps to maintain or improve health. It also involves seeking out resources, such as medical professionals or support groups, when needed.

Madiskarte thinking can be applied to health and wellness by setting clear and specific goals, visualizing positive outcomes, practicing gratitude, being resourceful and creative with nutrition and exercise, and taking responsibility for one's own health. By applying these principles, individuals can create a positive and healthy environment for the mind and body, and attract positive experiences and outcomes.

Madiskarte in Health and Wellness

Madiskarte, a Filipino term for strategic thinking or being resourceful, can also be applied to health and wellness. The Law of Attraction, a principle that states that like attracts like, can be utilized to achieve optimal health and wellness. By applying *Madiskarte* thinking, one can create a positive and healthy environment for the mind and body.

One of the fundamental aspects of *Madiskarte* thinking in health and wellness is setting clear and specific health goals. The Law of Attraction works by focusing on the positive outcome and energy that a person wants to attract. Therefore, by setting clear and specific health goals, an individual can focus their energy and attention on achieving those goals. For example, if a person wants to lose weight, they should set a specific goal, such as losing 10 pounds in two months. This will help them stay motivated and focused on their objective.

Visualization is another important technique that can be used in *Madiskarte* thinking for health and wellness. Visualization is the process of imagining oneself in a particular situation, which helps the brain to create a positive image of that situation. By visualizing oneself as healthy, happy, and vibrant, the brain can create positive neural pathways that can lead to actual physical changes in the body. This technique can be used to overcome obstacles, reduce stress, and increase motivation.

Gratitude is also an essential component of *Madiskarte* thinking in health and wellness. Gratitude is the act of recognizing and appreciating the positive aspects of life. By focusing on the good things, an individual can create positive energy and attract more positive experiences. Practicing gratitude can also reduce stress, boost the immune system, and improve mental health.

In addition, *Madiskarte* thinking can also be applied to nutrition and exercise. By being resourceful and creative, one can find healthy and enjoyable ways to nourish and move their body. For example, instead of relying on fast food for convenience, a person can prepare healthy meals in advance and bring them to work. Or, instead of feeling obligated to go to the gym, a person can find physical activities they enjoy, such as hiking, dancing, or swimming.

Finally, *Madiskarte* thinking in health and wellness also involves taking responsibility for one's own health. This means being aware of one's body and taking proactive steps to maintain or improve health. It also involves seeking out resources, such as medical professionals or support groups, when needed.

Madiskarte thinking can be applied to health and wellness by setting clear and specific goals, visualizing positive outcomes, practicing gratitude, being resourceful and creative with nutrition and exercise, and taking responsibility for one's own health. By applying these principles, individuals can create a positive and healthy environment for the mind and body, and attract positive experiences and outcomes.

Conclusion

"*Madiskarte*: Strategic Thinking with the Law of Attraction in Mind" is a powerful guide to developing a positive mindset, setting goals, and achieving success in all areas of life. Throughout this book, readers have learned about the Law of Attraction and its role in manifesting abundance, success, and happiness. They have discovered how to use visualization, positive thinking, and gratitude to attract their desired outcomes.

In Part I, readers have learned about the science behind the Law of Attraction and how their thoughts and emotions influence their reality. In Part II, they have learned how to apply the Law of Attraction in strategic thinking by defining their goals and dreams, creating a vision board, and visualizing their success. Part III has provided strategies for embracing abundance thinking, overcoming limiting beliefs, cultivating a positive mindset, and practicing gratitude and appreciation. Finally, in Part IV, readers have seen how *Madiskarte* thinking can be applied in various aspects of life, such as business and entrepreneurship, career and professional development, personal relationships, and health and wellness.

By embracing *Madiskarte* thinking, readers can transform their lives by manifesting their desires and achieving their goals. By focusing on the positive and visualizing their success, they can overcome limiting beliefs and cultivate a growth mindset. They can learn to appreciate the present moment, practice gratitude, and develop resilience and perseverance in the face of challenges.

"*Madiskarte*: Strategic Thinking with the Law of Attraction in Mind" is a valuable resource for anyone looking to improve their life, achieve their goals, and manifest abundance and happiness. By following the strategies outlined in this book, readers can develop a positive mindset and create the life they desire. With the Law of Attraction and *Madiskarte* thinking, anything is possible.

The Power of *Madiskarte*

Madiskarte is a strategic way of thinking that combines the principles of the Law of Attraction with practical action to achieve success and happiness in life. This approach emphasizes the importance of mindset, visualization, and taking deliberate action to achieve one's goals and dreams. By cultivating a positive, abundance-based mindset and using visualization techniques, individuals can attract the outcomes they desire and take action to make those desires a reality.

The power of *Madiskarte* lies in its ability to help individuals overcome limiting beliefs and negative thought patterns that hold them back from achieving their full potential. By focusing on positive outcomes and taking deliberate action towards achieving them, individuals can create a positive feedback loop that reinforces their belief in their ability to achieve their goals. The Law of Attraction, which states that like attracts like, supports this approach by emphasizing the importance of thoughts and emotions in shaping one's reality.

In essence, *Madiskarte* is a holistic approach to personal development that emphasizes the interconnectedness of mind, body, and spirit. By aligning these three components and focusing on positive outcomes, individuals can create a sense of purpose and direction in their lives that leads to greater happiness and success. This approach is not limited to any specific area of life, but can be applied to any aspect, including business, career, relationships, and health and wellness.

One of the key elements of *Madiskarte* is the use of visualization techniques to create a clear picture of one's desired outcome. By visualizing oneself in the desired state, individuals can create a sense of certainty and conviction that reinforces their belief in their ability to achieve their goals. This technique is often used in combination with affirmations and other positive self-talk to reinforce positive beliefs and reinforce a positive self-image.

Another important aspect of *Madiskarte* is the emphasis on taking deliberate action towards one's goals. This involves setting specific, measurable goals and creating a plan of action to achieve them. By breaking down larger goals into smaller, more manageable steps, individuals can avoid feeling overwhelmed and stay focused on their desired outcome.

Overall, the power of *Madiskarte* lies in its ability to help individuals take control of their lives and create the outcomes they desire. By combining the principles of the Law of Attraction with practical action and a positive mindset, individuals can create a sense of purpose and direction in their lives that leads to greater happiness and success. Whether applied to business, career, relationships, or health and wellness, *Madiskarte* offers a powerful approach to personal development that can help individuals achieve their full potential and live a fulfilling, meaningful life.

Putting *Madiskarte* into Practice

Madiskarte is a concept that emphasizes strategic thinking and the Law of Attraction in achieving success and reaching one's goals. It involves a mindset shift that focuses on abundance, positivity, and taking intentional actions towards one's dreams. While the idea of *Madiskarte* may sound simple, putting it into practice can be challenging. In this essay, we will discuss practical tips for putting *Madiskarte* into practice and achieving success in various aspects of life.

The first step to putting *Madiskarte* into practice is defining your goals and dreams. To do this effectively, it's important to be specific and clear about what you want to achieve. Write down your goals and break them down into smaller, actionable steps. This will help you create a roadmap to success and keep you focused on your end goal. When defining your goals, it's also essential to visualize yourself achieving them. This helps to strengthen your belief in your ability to achieve your goals, which is crucial for using the Law of Attraction.

Once you have defined your goals, the next step is to create a vision board. A vision board is a powerful tool for manifesting your dreams and keeping them at the forefront of your mind. It involves creating a visual representation of your goals and desires, using images and words that resonate with you. By looking at your vision board every day, you reinforce your belief in your ability to achieve your goals and attract the resources you need to make them a reality.

Another essential component of *Madiskarte* is cultivating a positive mindset. This involves being aware of your thoughts and actively replacing negative thoughts with positive ones. Instead of dwelling on what could go wrong, focus on what could go right. Practice gratitude by focusing on what you have rather than what you lack. When faced with challenges, view them as opportunities to learn and grow, rather than setbacks.

To practice *Madiskarte* effectively, it's also important to take action towards your goals. This involves breaking down your goals into actionable steps and taking intentional actions towards them every day. Remember that the Law of Attraction works in conjunction with your actions. You can't simply wish for success and expect it to come to you. You have to put in the work and take intentional actions towards your goals.

In addition to taking action, it's also important to embrace abundance thinking. This means recognizing that there is an abundance of resources, opportunities, and possibilities available to you. Instead of operating from a scarcity mindset, where you feel like there is never enough, embrace the idea that there is always more than enough. This helps to open up your mind to new opportunities and possibilities, which can lead to greater success and fulfillment.

Finally, it's essential to practice resilience and perseverance. This involves being able to bounce back from setbacks and failures and continuing to move forward towards your goals. Remember that success is not always linear, and setbacks are a natural part of the process. Use setbacks as an opportunity to learn and grow, and keep moving forward towards your goals.

Madiskarte is a powerful tool for achieving success in various aspects of life. By defining your goals, creating a vision board, cultivating a positive mindset, taking action, embracing abundance thinking, and practicing resilience and perseverance, you can put *Madiskarte* into practice and achieve your dreams. Remember that *Madiskarte* involves a mindset shift, so it may take time and effort to fully integrate it into your life. However, with practice and perseverance, you can harness the power of *Madiskarte* and achieve success in all areas of your life.

Embracing a *Madiskarte* Mindset

The term "*Madiskarte*" is a Filipino term that roughly translates to strategic thinking, resourcefulness, and creativity. In the context of the Law of Attraction, *Madiskarte* is the ability to use your thoughts and emotions to manifest your desires and achieve your goals. Embracing a *Madiskarte* mindset involves cultivating a positive and empowered attitude towards life, taking ownership of your thoughts and actions, and developing resilience in the face of challenges.

One of the core principles of the Law of Attraction is the idea that your thoughts and emotions create your reality. If you focus on negative thoughts and feelings, you will attract negative experiences into your life. Conversely, if you focus on positive thoughts and feelings, you will attract positive experiences into your life. Embracing a *Madiskarte* mindset involves taking ownership of your thoughts and emotions and consciously directing them towards your desired outcomes.

One of the key components of a *Madiskarte* mindset is a belief in abundance. This means that you believe that there is an abundance of opportunities, resources, and possibilities available to you. When you have a mindset of abundance, you are more likely to take risks, try new things, and pursue your goals with confidence. This mindset also helps you to focus on what you want, rather than what you don't want, and to see setbacks and challenges as opportunities for growth and learning.

Another important aspect of a *Madiskarte* mindset is the ability to overcome limiting beliefs. Limiting beliefs are negative beliefs that we hold about ourselves, our abilities, and the world around us. These beliefs can hold us back from achieving our goals and living our best lives. Embracing a *Madiskarte* mindset means recognizing these limiting beliefs and actively working to replace them with more empowering beliefs that support our goals and dreams.

Cultivating a positive mindset is also an essential component of a *Madiskarte* mindset. This involves focusing on the positive aspects of your life, practicing gratitude and appreciation, and surrounding yourself with positive and supportive people. A positive mindset helps you to stay motivated and inspired, even in the face of challenges, and allows you to approach your goals with a sense of joy and enthusiasm.

Finally, developing resilience and perseverance is crucial for anyone looking to embrace a *Madiskarte* mindset. Resilience is the ability to bounce back from setbacks and challenges, while perseverance is the ability to stay focused and committed to your goals over the long term. These qualities help you to stay motivated and focused, even when faced with obstacles, and allow you to keep moving forward towards your desired outcomes.

Embracing a *Madiskarte* mindset involves cultivating a positive and empowered attitude towards life, taking ownership of your thoughts and actions, and developing resilience in the face of challenges. By practicing *Madiskarte* thinking, you can harness the power of the Law of Attraction to manifest your desires and achieve your goals, in all areas of your life.